No Filter

LaShawnda Nimox

BookLeaf
Publishing

India | USA | UK

Presentation by *BookLeaf Publishing*

Web: www.bookleafpub.com

E-mail: info@bookleafpub.com

ISBN: 9789360945312

First edition 2024

DEDICATION

This book is dedicated to anyone that has experienced trauma in any space where they were made to feel small, silenced or unseen. I hope this book gives you the strength and permission you need to speak your truth unapologetically and with No Filter.

ACKNOWLEDGEMENT

I would like to acknowledge my children Jalen, Cherish and Bryce they are the motivation and the reason I do anything. I would like to thank my 5th grade teacher Ms. Adams because she always pushed me because she saw something in me long before I saw it in myself. I would like to thank my Uncle Danny and my Aunt Sandra they put books in my hand and I've lived a thousand lives because of it. To my sister Enjoli (Le-Le) if a ride or die was a person it is definitely you. To my cousin Molly thanks for all your support and encouragement its great to have a big sister. To my Best Friend since 6th grade, Kira thank you for laughing, traveling, motivating and reminding me that God has my back. To my best friend Tan thanks for being the organizer, supporter and glue that holds everybody down and together. To my friend Nicoya, we may not talk all the time, we may not get to hang out much but when we do its always a good time and feels like we never missed a beat. To my friend Terry thanks for being a listening ear, always being honest and a safe space to escape when its needed most. To my Malone Center family thanks for allowing me to be innovative and giving me the freedom to create with no ceilings. Honorable mention to my exe's thank you I couldn't see it then but I see it was just what I needed for this moment. To those that might not like me or prefer not to get to know me it sucks for you and I hope you deal with whatever issue you have within yourself cuz that's definitely personal. To my parents I appreciate the things you have done and for doing your best. To CRCL, the place that holds a special place in my heart, the place that made being a kid worthwhile. I am forever grateful to be a product of that environment especially during the time frame that I attended. It was home. To my amazing grandmother Norma, its not enough words to express everything you've been to me and i literally mean you've been everything, your love and wisdom I will cherish forever it is Priceless and I am forever grateful to have a praying grandmother. To Mental Health I see you, I acknowledge you and I address you accordingly. To anyone fighting a silent battle with illness, domestic violence, suicide, depression, homelessness or fear You Are Not Alone and You Can Do This. To myself, stay prayerful, stay innovative, optimistic, speak over yourself and live life with No Filter.

Please use 988 as a resource for suicide
prevention or if you need someone to talk to
because you are not alone.

PREFACE

 These writings are where I have found solace while navigating life. The truth is trauma doesn't have favorites, it doesn't care the amount of money, fame, location, gender, or ethnicity. We hear people say "if it was me, I would've" or my favorite "couldn't be me" easy to say when you are a visitor and not a dweller. We all have had moments where we have either been silenced or have had to think long and hard before speaking whether that's because of work, abuse, or backlash and it is exhausting. So at this moment while you are reading this book I want you to know that I see you and I challenge you to begin to take up space, embrace your Trauma, speak your Truth, celebrate your Triumphs and do it all with No Filter.

I don't Know Who Needs to Hear This but...

I don't know who needs to hear this but you aren't the only person having a bad day.

I don't know who needs to hear this but I see you and you are loved.

I don't know who needs to hear this but that is your child's mother or the mother of your children not your baby mama.

I don't know who needs to hear this but that is your child's father or the father of your children not your baby daddy.

I don't know who needs to hear this but if that Man or Woman said they don't want a relationship and you do, don't entertain him find someone that wants what you want.

I don't know who needs to hear this but staying in a relationship or marriage for the sake of the children is unhealthy.

I don't know who needs to hear this but your
kids hear you arguing.

I don't know who needs to hear this but kids
need to be heard.

I don't know who needs to hear this but don't
respond, ignoring is much more powerful.

I don't know who needs to hear this but your
kids don't need another pair of Jordan's and they
don't even know who he is.

I don't know who needs to hear this but your
child needs to read at home.

I don't know who needs to hear this but go to
your child's basketball and football games.

I don't know who needs to hear this but Let that
man see his kids.

I don't know who needs to hear this but God
wouldn't send you somebody else's man.

I don't know who needs to hear this but stop
calling them kids out of their name.

I don't know who needs to hear this but fix your crown.

I don't know who needs to hear this but take that trip.

I don't know who needs to hear this but your family is your trigger.

I don't know who needs to hear this but friends don't compete.

I don't know who needs to hear this but Leave.

I don't know who needs to hear this but you've heard "Sorry" for the last time.

I don't know who needs to hear this but you deserve to be loved.

I don't know who needs to hear this but Love doesn't hurt.

I don't know who needs to hear this but Forgive them and then Forgive yourself.

I don't know who needs to hear this but Spend time with your kids.

I don't know who needs to hear this but stop
taking advice from people whose situations are
worst then yours.

I don't know who needs to hear this but You Are
Amazing.

I don't know who needs to hear this but..... I
needed to hear this and You Do too.

Monsters Exist

We all have seen the movies of the child running
to their parents room in the middle of the night.
 Crying, panicking that something in their room
is not right.

The parents escort them back to bed to their own
space reassure them that there is nothing to be
afraid of because they will keep them safe.

Those are the monsters that we are told are not
real the thought is dismissed but jokes on them
because Monsters do exist.

The monster might come in the form of friends
and family they creep into your room with their
own agenda.

The teacher at school that was looking out for
you, she brought you to her class for a private
rendezvous.
You didn't know, you wasn't prepared to find out
that dreams can turn into nightmares.

The dad with a fist of fire toward the mother and
a tongue of knives toward the children all living
behind a wall of fear.
Do you still believe there are no monsters here.

The coach said you are the next G.O.A.T, then
her husband and children went missing and it
was Murder She Wrote.

A monster is as an imaginary creature, and some
things may not make much sense but takeaway
from this that Monsters most definitely Exist.

Hurt

The hurt, the exhaustion, the friction of pain
meeting pissed off.
I'm okay, yeah just fine that is probably the best
lie I keep selling to everybody.

My appearance says she's all together my insides
are fighting to find reason to be alive.
It is all misleading and confusing at best, I've
made my mind believe something my heart
keeps struggling with.

I am enough that's what I tell myself verbally but
silently I question if I ever will be.
 I can't seem to find my confidence and my
purpose. Who am I and am I capable of
experiencing true unconditional love.

Nobody warns of the hate you begin to feel of
the intesity to still have to be everything for
everybody and nothing to yourself while you
heal.

The immediate need of a break or a moment just
to cry to owe no loyalty and cut all ties.

The urge to burn others feelings cuz they don't
give a fuck about mine.

Tired of laying in the ashes of their apologies
wanting to grab their tongue in my hand as it has
only told lies.

They continue to look at you in your face and
not care about your pain not knowing you are
the thunder, and that you are the rain.

To hurt you like you hurt me and take another
between my legs and not have a memory or
thought of you in my head.
To place your eyes on a pedestal and have you
watch me cheat not just my body but all of me.

The damage is done, self esteem has taken a hit,
do I go or do I stay and try to fix this.
What is broken, will this work?
Can anything good come out of all this Hurt!

Drunk Mind Sober Heart

I wish you could see the transition from sober to
drunk, from laughter, jokes and hugs to yells and
nit picking on everything.

Your face changes, you turn from soft and gentle
to aggressive and harsh and every conversation
like liquor goes from light to dark.

It's like devils advocate when there is liquor
involved its like watching a brand new candle
melt from beauty to beast in a manner of
minutes.
You don't see the issue but we all relive it.

The stories start about violence or childhood
fights, your corner dreams and tales of youthful
nights.

Then begins the laughter and the dramatizations,
yelling to get your point across in every
conversation.
Then comes the threats or thing you've been
thinking about for a while. You talk about the
kids being lazy and how I never smile.

Let's not forget you telling that you've been on your own since you were sixteen a so called abusive mom, absent father an ongoing theme clearly there is trauma that is unseen.

You don't make yourself available or apart of the family team but always appear over the top, overbearing and just so mean.

Your always right, we're always wrong, you're always gone and we're always home.

Maybe its not you, maybe its us. Our sober world and your drunk one doesn't match up. Sober makes you feel the pain and Alcohol makes you numb.

I know there is so many things that play a part but if there is nothing else I know from experience is that a drunk mind often speaks a sober heart.

Safe Space

Some people when asked where is their safe
space may respond by saying home or in their
bedroom, some might even go as far as to say
their parents house or with a friend or family
member but for me that space is internal.

Underneath my skin, beyond the pulse of my
heart beat their lies my feelings, my thoughts,
my fears and sometimes my goals.

The space is starting to be cluttered I have boxes
and boxes full of sentences that I didn't say,
thoughts I didn't share, emotions that I forgot to
feel or didn't allow myself to feel. If it were a
way to take a glimpse or peak into the space I
am not sure you could get through the door.

I have become a hoarder of feelings and I never
meant for it to get this bad but somehow,
unconsciously it started with me throwing one
feeling in and closing the door but little did I
know the door didn't close all the way because
before I knew it I had began to go to this place at
least once per week and then it turned into daily

and soon it became open 24 hours and 7 days a week and I had become a regular customer.

In this space its too many boxes and bags to count I know its overflowing because I keep trying to put some stuff in it and now the door won't close. I keep pushing the door and it won't latch so now its time to start the cleaning out my space but it seems like I forgot how to clean it. I can't bring myself to enter the room to read the labels of the boxes in my safe space.

Some of the boxes I don't need to open I can just read the label and know exactly why it was put away. There are boxes there with my insecurities the feelings of not being enough, there are tears in here because of the amount of times I have wanted to cry but had to hold them back. At some point in time I put my courage in a box and even my voice I remember when I lost my voice.

There were several experiences that contributed to the box with my voice, I remember the moment things went silent and I can still feel the air around me that day not knowing what to do I packaged it down and put it away.

Childhood wounds of presents instead of
presence emotionally detached parents. Scars
from unspoken words, lack of physical touch,
screaming silently in a space where you go with
the flow and you know what you know but the
only problem is nobody is paying attention to
the kid that needs more then basic needs so
another box is added and its labeled
Miscellaneous from childhood.

Family says they are a listening ear but they
leave out that they have a judgmental eye and
heart so there are numerous boxes of family or
"family".

The words "I Don't Know" well that's true
sometimes "I really don't know". Question:
Why do you stay? Answer: I don't know.
Question: What do you want? Answer: I don't
know.

There is also a corner of boxes that are labeled "I
wonder" to represent all those instances of
wonder. Wonder has been an interesting battle
such wondrous thoughts such as "I wonder if
he's cheating... I wonder what it feels like to
have flowers or chocolates delivered just
because, to get a text to say "thinking of you

everyday.. to have the people Show Up for you, I wonder....

I glance around quickly and notice the boxes of disappointments piled up high those times I thought the people that cared the most would speak up but they watched me suffer from the side line. When you seem like more of an inconvenience that your own parent gives you the side eye. I decided that I wouldn't allow anymore room for disappointments because I would no longer depend on anybody but me.

I scan the space again and see along the sealed boxes labeled Passive, Overwhelmed, Tired, Alone and Betrayed I stare and realize so many boxes of negativity and at this moment I open the door as wide as I can with tears in my eyes, I kneel with hands closed and pray.

I open my eyes and open the door as far as I can and I begin to remove each box one by one throwing them out of the space they have claimed for so many years. In a short amount of time I was able to stand in the middle of this space and spin in a circle, the space was empty free of clutter and I could breathe.

I knew keep down inside that I would fill this space again but this time I am filling this space with boxes full of Love, Happiness, Peace and Positivity. The place I resort to when I need reassurance and confidence.

It is my own, I am in charge and I opened an empty box and labeled it "Self Love" and placed it in the middle of the floor of my newly remodeled safe space.

Nowhere

We can't go nowhere together it never turns out
well, its always something that turns a good
night into my own personal Hell.
So aggressive, possessive and overbearing at
times used to be a good look now it just too
much in my book.

Aruguments, fights, side eyes and dysfunction
isn't my idea of fun but then again growing up is
not for everyone.

Aggressive and Assertive, Protective and
Overbearing and most importantly Afraid and
Safe. Looking over your face as it changes in
time one drink, two drink I know the monster is
coming in a short amount of time.
I know that Love is still somewhere inside but I
watch it grow dim cup after cup until it has
nowhere to reside.

I know where drunken souls and darkness meet,
I feel it in the air and I know where it exists I
don't want to be there. The space seems cold the
walls seem close it becomes too much to bare so

lets save ourself the trouble stay inside and
choose to go Nowhere.

17

My Voice

Not sure when it happened, can't really pinpoint
the time, month or year. I can't remember if it
was by choice, fear or force but I know that I
have lost my voice.

The constant chatter in my head of things I want
to say but for some reason I choose to stay quiet
instead. Somewhere in this journey I learned to
be silent and let things pass maybe its all the
yelling and name calling that I'd much rather
pass.

The things you settle for even though you know
you don't deserve it, constant thoughts that this
just can't be it.

My Physical appearance doesn't reflect my
emotional stability at all.
Everyday I'm breaking and I know at any
moment I am going to crumble and fall.

Have the words but not the voice I have the
heart but not the force so quiet and quieter I get
until I disappear then off to the shower I go to
shed my tears.

When did I become afraid, when did I become
nothing to myself, when did my Peace become
equivalent to death.

Something clicked it just happened overnight,
the feeling of self worth and I decided to make a
choice so here I am entering the beginning of the
season of Reclaiming my voice.

Birthday Licks

March 14th is my birthday. It is the day that I
was born and coincidently the day I survived.
3.14 how excited was I until the day ended with
a black eye.

From yelling in the car because you felt a way
turning everything into an argument on my dam
birthday. Another night cut short cuz you
couldn't handle yourself that is what you do,
made a night that was about me all about you.

Yelling and screaming in my face being called
so many Bitches was hard for my mental to take.
I told you to just leave I would be okay then I
felt your hand from behind slap me across my
face. I was at a disadvantage, it was a bitch
move my back was turned its the last thing I'd
expect from you.

You pulled me down, I fell to the bed. I clawed
at your face, then a punch to the side of my
head, a blow to my lip. At this point I'm kicking
and screaming can somebody help. You've
pinned me down hand chocking me I look

through tears as the man that says he loves me
face disappears.

This can't be him not the father of my children,
not the love of my life, not the man that asked
me to be his wife. Blood from my lip staining
my clothes I peer to the side and our daughter is
at the door.

You get up she's there at my side then she
disappears to her room where I assumed she'd go
and hide. A blood stained dress a bruised eye
and thumb prints to my neck. I had to be done
this time because death had to be next.

Banging at the front and back door as I wipe
blood from my lip its the police that I didn't call
here. Death to my confidence and death to my
pride and death to Love and any emotions
inside.

The bruises were beyond what the eyes could
see, I had internally died there was no more to
me. it was all gone I couldn't come back I told
myself he's a good person he didn't mean to do
that. I picked up the pieces and try to glue
things back together but everything became a
trigger.

The paranoia set in. My anxiety through the roof
and I could hear my heart skip a beat when he
entered the room. A blank smile, no sleep I was
defeated, scared to have a voice or an opinion.

There were always other women you entertained
and I wondered if you ever hit them the same.
The thoughts of self harm, not wanting to be
alive crept into my mind wondering when you'd
notice since you never came home half the time.

It hurt, it hurt all of it hurt to be in sunlight and
still be in the dark and have a broken spirit,
broken relationship and a broken heart. Too
much to carry the weight made me sick you
managed to give literal meaning to the words
birthday licks.

Triggered

In the strangest of ways, on the strangest of
days, inside something is brewing, I feel it and I
cave. Trauma is something so unique it lingers,
it creeps in places you thought was safe, it
occupies a permanent space in your mind, it
comes and goes at different points in time.

If you've gone through something traumatic
there are things that have you on edge, its simple
to some but a big deal for you, it snaps your
body back to whatever experiences you went
through.

These Triggers they haunt and rent space in your
mind, it shakes us and pulls us and disrupts our
state of mind. Raising your voice puts me on
edge, that car you drive isn't fun to be a
passenger anymore and please, please don't slam
the front door.

I know, I know it has been 6 months or more and
I thought I'd be over it before the end of the year
but Triggers keep happening and my body
screams in fear.

That dress despite how cute it is I can't see it
clearly I only see blood and tears, the collar with
the blood stains and a small button that no
longer exists looking at it hurts me to death I
have to look away quick to catch my breath.

The earrings bought out of love so tiny and
powerful I hold them in my hand and try to put
them in my ear then my head begins to hurt and
my eyes shed tears.

I'm not sure I'll ever be content sitting on the
edge of the bed I hear whispers of those awful,
hurtful things your mouth said.

That mirror shows a reflection of me but I look
in it and see the bloody face of a woman made to
feel small and I've tried and can't get this image
out of my head at all. So all these things they
trigger me , they suffocate my thoughts, they
crowd my space.

I pray, ask for peace and I close my eyes and
wait for God to whisper, 'I have you my child,
your are free from your Triggers".

It Should Be You

That one night changed my life. The problem is
I keep trying to forgive and forget but I am
constantly triggered. I try to say they are old
wounds now. It's been months I need to get over
it somehow.

Every now and then I can taste the blood on my
lip, I go in the bathroom to confirm its just my
mind playing tricks. I don't get why this time is
different I think it hurt so much more because I
saw my child hurting at the door.

The date is a game changer in itself, it was
special day for me a memorable moment in time,
its the date I was born the date etched in time, its
the date I was born and now coincidentally the
day I believe I died inside.

I want you to go but strangely I want you to stay
its an argument in my head every single day.
My only drive is my kids I won't leave them to
mourn instead we will cope, but then you raise
your voice and it causes me to choke.

I've chosen life, I've chosen to heal you don't own me and nobody knows or should tell me how to feel. I keep wondering why I am so afraid to fly, I love you, I love you but I don't know why.

This isn't healthy, I understand that hurt people hurt people but when does it stop. Riddled with blood, bruises and cuts this is just a bunch of foolery. Now my life is literally a lifetime movie.

There is something in me dying to shake free, I can't put a finger on it but it is challenging me. I take the jail phone calls because I seem to still care for you and you assume since I haven't left that I'll always be there.

This time is different, the pain, the hurt the space seems to be cursed. This time isn't about who apologizes first, I don't know if I can get past this and I can't with you near I can't get over this and I shouldn't have to but if anyone should leave it should be you.

Rain in the forecast

Hey you, yeah you, you think you can just glide
through life. You think you can lay up, fuck up,
and stay out all night?

Man be for real you think you gonna keep acting
up, tears I shed over what led to a bed that your
are comfortable in to lay within a pair of legs
that spread open but you crossed the line cuz I
am far from your mind and those legs aren't
mine but you, you are mine.

Time and time again when I knew not to let you
in despite the thoughts deep within saying don't
do it again and again I take you in with open
arms only to open healed wounds and leave new
scars.

You see it was supposed to be different you say
you only wanted me I saw the other chick and
felt confused immediately. My self -esteem is
shot but she is not hot, I mean they cuz its
always more then one, they are not hot. But if
its opened legs these days you don't have to go
far and using your head can keep your house

fed, a warm body in the bed, a wife at home being misled.

We play the fool all too often tracks of tears on our cheeks, hurt in our heart, world on our shoulders, trust diminished, self esteem lost, enough is enough but to him you will never be enough but to you sis Are you enough?

You've decided its time to choose you, light the candle , strike the match, pour the gasoline and watch the fire burn. The moment when things shift in her favor , the world looks different, she feels free and guess what you're not in it.

It is peace she has found and decided upon, she forgives you but decides it is time to move on. You yell horrible words in her direction, tell her she'll never find nobody better, tell her she won't get her shit together, you say the grass aint greener on the other side well that may be true but its more then grass that we seek and while you've been busy messing around, picking different women up and taking them down. You couldn't keep up with all of her pain, you created these storm clouds now you mad that it rained.

Soul Tie

What do yo do when the feelings are there. You have history together, a friendship, magical moments in time. You agreed not to care, this was fun but its turned into a matter of the heart and the request of friends with benefits is now unfair.

He's truth, peace and your fresh air and you've both caught feelings and you both know but you've agreed to not let them show. It seems so different the second time around you feel each others connection its no denying it now.

Its hard to date because you're looking for each other in other people, the fire is still there but nobody will strike the match, is it fear of what could be but we just stand by and play the game of wait and see.

There's a formula to the chemistry, its madness to know the answer only equals us. The math is mathing its ignorance to the math that has made things tough.

Checking in on each other just enough to leave
room for an excuse that you were thinking of
them and they were thinking of you. One thing
always lead to another in conversation and in
person its love or at best it feels that way but you
both deny it again and silently agree to push
those feelings away.

He could be your person and you could be his as
well you both are living through your own
personal, mental hell. Calling it a friendship
puts you both at ease, you believe the
relationship you live in your mind, only to waste
more time living your truth with what is nothing
more than a soul tie.

Real Talk

Looks like America knocked on America's door,
waking up the silent hallways and shaking the
columns on the Capitol floor.

You didn't hear the peaceful protest of the people
when the law had George Floyd's neck but it
ruffled your feathers cuz somebody put their feet
on Nancy Pelosi's desk.

The nerve the audacity how disgusted are we
that you carry a flag while you destroy
democracy.

Was anyone else impressed with the amount of
restraint nobody got a bullet to the back and no
hashtags pleading to say their names. No pepper
spray, no tear gas, barricades or even a fence but
a noose hanging outside apparently for Mike
Pence.

I thought Blue Lives Mattered, oh wait all lives
matter so could someone explain that our fight is
different, we are not the same.

You didn't shoot them like you shoot us, you didn't police them like you police us and we want to know why a man walked out the front door with a podium without even a taser to the back or a side eye.

In a bunker refusing to send help with people lives at stake crying nothings fair like a toddler whose mom won't let him have anymore cake. Let's just put it out there Obama could have never I mean he barely made it out alive after the whole tan suit scandal.

Next time y'all have a house party can we come, hell we can't walk our own neighborhoods I know we wouldn't make it past the steps but maybe we can bbq on the White House lawn. Sorry can't do that either Karen keeps reporting it to law enforcement.

In the words of Malcom X the chickens have come home to roost there's two different Americas all living under one roof, and sadly the line has officially been drawn the question now is Which side of history will you choose to be on?

Agree to Disagree

They stand together ready to argue and chant
"all lives matter" and nobody disagrees with that
so does that logic not apply when the person is
black? Just need a moment of clarity, lets take a
look at this issue in its true state since this topic
repeatedly seems to be up for debate. Divided
households, friendships at risk, Black America
waiting on a new Schindler's list. they stand
together and they chant "all lives matter".

Well lets give America a second look did all
lives matter on that dreadful day at Sandy Hook?
On that awful day was it up for debate, did you
hear anyone or the slightest bit of chatter while
all around America hearts shattered. Nobody
thought to argue that "all kindergarteners
matter".

I think we can agree and lets be exact it wasn't
all kindergarteners that were under attack but
you still felt the pain and was in disbelief for the
disregard of lives of those little girls and boys
but were their lives valued higher than that of
George Floyd.

And still you say "all lives matter" well yes they do and I wonder the backlash you'd get if you showed up at Stoneman Douglas on February 14th and told them "all schools matter" too. Seems to me if all lives matter when any one of those lives is under attack we should all stand together and fight back.

 Leave it up to America to make tragedy selfish instead of acknowledge when a group of people are under attack, we need more accountability aren't we tired of hash tags.

In That Order

The arrival of family and friends at the park, the
bar be que grills still smoldering after dark. The
lawn chairs all facing the sky, waiting for the
loud bang and beautiful colors to catch your eye.

The sound of laughter, music and children
running to get a closer view this is July 4th and
it's the only Independence Day I ever knew.

What is this Juneteenth in my African American
study course you mean we weren't free on July
4th?

The nerve of America and the history books, you
sold us a story, dressed it up real nice put a bow
on it and thought we wouldn't think twice.

 Your track record with the African American
race has always been built on YOUR truth its
Happy Juneteenth from here on out in fact July
4th who?

The movement, the struggle, the fight to be free.
Juneteenth is our victory.

Juneteenth means growth and resilience in a space full of resistance.

It means peaceful protest in hallways of a house that doesn't welcome you to a seat, only to find out you'll be the one responsible for their accountability.

Juneteenth is a reminder of Freedom, Voice, inclusion and hope. It holds cops accountable, it makes my hair a crown, it makes us take up space, it makes us loud and proud.

 It is the cloud of protection, it is the fight in and around me, it is struggle and unity, it is Black History it can't be erased it is not Critical Race Theory.

June 19, 1865, Juneteenth, Freedom was granted, Freedom is the power or right to act, speak, or think as one wants without hindrance or restraint and it was awarded so my response to America is in that ORDER!

Russell Wilson

Have you put away your childish things? All the
stages of life, we had those things, participated
in things, brought alongs some things or shed
some things cuz the new level of life didn't
include some things or people if we are being
real.

Some friendships didn't make it, some family
got left but some of us accidentally carried a
seasonal person into our current season and he
has caused us nothing but hell. We turned up in
our 20's, The Chicago streets made me but I am
moving into my 40's and that mumble rap isn't
for me.

Now I'm on my grown woman shit while there is
still a hint of ratchet in me I need a grown man
with a hint of street that can get suited up and is
able to feed my soul rather than run the streets,
party all night that shit is old.

To each its own, I don't think its too much to
ask. I'm looking toward the future not the ghosts
of future's past. I heard you can't raise a man

and really I have no time to because at that point
you're my son and I already have two.

I get it if you're not down or all the way in but
I'm speaking over my future, I'm ready and
waiting for my own Russell Wilson.

Give Yourself Permission

Give yourself permission to hurt, it's okay you
won't hurt forever.
Give yourself permission to feel overwhelmed it
happens and it will make you better.
Give yourself permission to laugh out loud,
sometimes it soothes the smallest of fears.
Give yourself permission to be angry but decide
when to let the anger pass.
Give yourself permission to take a break, you
need one and you earned it.
Give yourself permission to make mistakes then
you know what not to do again.
Give yourself permission to take cry, cleanse
your soul and start fresh.
Give yourself permission to forgive, it is for you
and you only.
Give yourself permission to be loved, Its waiting
on you and its special.
Give yourself permission to give your
permission and the rest will fall in line.......

90's soundtrack

The music of the 90's a time was had. The time
when love songs gave you chills and lyrics told a
story that would last a lifetime.

Hip hop made you think and had a message for
anyone that would listen and R&B set the mood
and made you appreciate the musician.

The vocals, the instruments, the visuals shouldn't
be remissed it was a time of art, creativity a
certain finesse wrapped in a bow with a kiss.

The songs that we had 4 or 5 artist on one track
can we rewind the times please take me back.

You couldn't purchase an explicit album unless
you were an adult it was the rule so you sang
and rapped radio versions because that is all you
knew.

It was just different compared to today and its
referred to as throwback but just know there is
no today's music without that 90's soundtrack.

From one educator to another

From one educator to another don't give up on
them they need you. The parents don't know it
yet but they need you too. You're administration
is making decisions that you know first hand
won't work seems like an uphill battle but keep
fighting.

Stay the course, keep your ear to the ground and
yesterday was hard but tomorrow will be
different. Just stand firm that you are making a
difference, I guarantee you're at least impacting
one. But that kid that curses you out everyday
just acknowledge that he is communicating.

The kid that has his hoodie on and head down
just a light tap on the shoulder lets him know
you see him and that touch alone are your words
for the day.

The kid that is attentive, follows directions, and
listens all too well may have something to prove
so don't just move on without explanation.

The kid that's sleeping in your class today its not disruptive but ask about it one on one later you might get the answer you are looking for.

Every now and then get on their level, use their language, laugh with them, show no reaction to everything, sit with them, show up for them because as tough as they are they see you and I know it is HARD but from one educator to another DON'T GIVE UP.

Time

We look at the time throughout the day, its a system put in place to keep things on track from day to day. It is also the very thing we make the mistake of thinking we have a lot of.

We under estimate our time with friends and family. We get busy with work, busy with distractions and before we know it something happens to remind us that time matters.

I challenge you to use your time wisely, use it with those that matter, use it to its full capacity and make each minute priceless because if there is one thing you don't have a lot of is TIME!

Get you a friend

Get you a friend that answers whenever you call.
Get you a friend that will call you out when you
are wrong.
Get you a friend that will be honest with you, a
friend that is modest, blunt and straightforward
with you.
Get you a friend that prays with and for you. A
friend that doesn't just look at you but actually
sees you.
A friend that will listen even when there is
nothing to listen to.
A friend that despite who comes along
consistently chooses you.
Get you a friend that shows up for you, that will
cry, drink wine and laugh at you too.
Get you a friend that is motivated and motivates
you, supports your dream even when its crazy,
wild and not realistic.
Get you a friend to share stories and create
memories.
Get you a friend that stands with you, that will
join in any shenanigans that involve you.
Get you a friend a real friend because it is
priceless.

If you don't have one already Go Get You A
Friend.

45